Apple watch series

10 user guide for

seniors

EUGENIA BARBER

Copyright

Table of Content

Introduction

1.1 What is the Apple Watch Series 10?

1.2 Key Features Overview

1.3 How This Guide Helps Seniors

Chapter 1

Getting Started

Unboxing and Setting Up Your Apple Watch

Pairing Your Apple Watch with Your iPhone

Adjusting the Watch Band

Chapter 2

Understanding the Basics

Overview of the Apple Watch Buttons and Touchscreen

Navigating the Watch Face

Understanding the Digital Crown and Side Button

Chapter 3

Personalizing Your Apple Watch

Changing the Watch Face

Adding and Managing Complications

Adjusting Display Brightness and Text Size

Chapter 4

Using Key Features

  Making and Receiving Calls

  Sending and Reading Messages

  Setting Alarms and Timers

  Using the Calendar

Chapter 5

Health and Fitness Features

  Tracking Your Steps and Activity Rings

  Using the Heart Rate Monitor

  Setting Fitness Goals

  Monitoring Sleep Patterns

Chapter 6

Staying Safe with Apple Watch

  Setting Up Fall Detection

  Using Emergency SOS

  Health Sharing with Loved Ones

Chapter 7

Staying Connected with Apple Watch Series 10

  Using Wi-Fi and Cellular Connections

Managing Notifications

Accessing Apps from the App Store

Chapter 8

Voice Assistance with Siri on Apple Watch Series 10

Activating Siri

Common Commands and How to Use Them

Troubleshooting Siri

Chapter 9

Customizing for Ease of Use on the Apple Watch Series 10

Accessibility Features

Enabling Zoom and VoiceOver

Simplifying Notifications

Chapter 10

Maintaining Your Apple Watch Series 10

Charging and Battery Tips

Cleaning and Caring for Your Watch

Updating watchOS

Chapter 11

Troubleshooting and Support

Common Issues and Solutions

Resetting Your Apple Watch

Getting Help from Apple Support

Tips and Tricks for Seniors

Maximizing Battery Life

Using the Watch as a Remote for Your iPhone

Exploring Hidden Features

Frequently Asked Questions (FAQs)

Conclusion and Final Tips

Introduction

1.1 What is the Apple Watch Series 10?

The Apple Watch Series 10 is the latest iteration of Apple's smartwatch lineup, offering cutting-edge technology and a sleek design that integrates seamlessly into everyday life. This device serves as a comprehensive tool for communication, health tracking, fitness monitoring, and entertainment, all conveniently worn on your wrist. With its intuitive interface and powerful features, the Series 10 is more than just a watch—it's a personal assistant, fitness coach, and health guardian in one compact package.

This smartwatch is tailored to meet the diverse needs of users, including seniors, by incorporating features that emphasize simplicity, safety, and accessibility. From tracking your heart rate to helping you stay connected with loved ones, the Apple Watch Series 10 brings the benefits of modern technology to your fingertips—or rather, your wrist. Its advanced sensors provide insights into your health, such as heart rate and blood oxygen levels, while its seamless integration with your iPhone allows you to make calls, send texts, and use apps without hassle.

For seniors, the Apple Watch Series 10 is particularly valuable as it enhances independence and peace of mind. Safety features like Fall Detection and Emergency SOS can automatically alert emergency services or designated contacts in case of an accident, offering reassurance in moments of uncertainty. The Series 10 embodies convenience and functionality, making it an ideal companion for navigating the challenges and opportunities of daily life.

1.2 Key Features Overview

The Apple Watch Series 10 stands out as a feature-rich device that caters to various needs, whether it's tracking your steps or staying connected on the go. Here's an overview of its standout capabilities:

- Always-On Display: The Series 10 boasts an advanced Always-On Retina display that's brighter and more energy-efficient, allowing you to see important information like time, notifications, or your activity metrics at a glance, even in bright sunlight.

- Advanced Health Monitoring: Equipped with sensors for heart rate monitoring, blood oxygen level tracking, and even ECG (electrocardiogram) readings, this smartwatch helps you keep tabs on vital health indicators. It also includes reminders to take medications, stay hydrated, or practice mindfulness.

- Fitness and Activity Tracking: The Activity Rings system motivates you to move, exercise, and stand throughout the day. The watch also tracks workouts, calories burned, and steps taken. It even offers specific modes for yoga, swimming, cycling, and more.

- Safety Features: Fall Detection can sense a hard fall and notify emergency services if you don't respond. Emergency SOS allows you to call for help instantly in urgent situations.

- Siri Voice Assistant: With Siri, you can use voice commands to set reminders, ask questions, or control smart devices in your home.

- Customizable Watch Faces: Choose from a wide variety of watch faces to suit your preferences. You can prioritize health data, calendars, or minimalist designs depending on your needs.

- Long Battery Life: The Series 10 offers extended battery life, ensuring that the watch stays active and reliable throughout your day.

Each feature is designed to be user-friendly and easily accessible, making it a perfect match for seniors who want to embrace technology without feeling overwhelmed.

1.3 How This Guide Helps Seniors

Navigating new technology can sometimes feel intimidating, especially if you're not familiar with the latest advancements. That's why this guide is tailored specifically for seniors, focusing on simplifying the Apple Watch Series 10 experience. Here's how it will assist you:

1. Clear Instructions: Each chapter includes step-by-step guidance for setting up, customizing, and using your Apple Watch. Detailed illustrations and straightforward explanations ensure that even first-time users can follow along effortlessly.

2. Senior-Friendly Tips: Throughout the guide, you'll find tips to help you adapt the watch to your preferences, such as increasing text size, enabling voice commands, or setting up emergency contacts. Accessibility features like Voiceover and zoom make the watch more intuitive and enjoyable to use.

3. Health and Safety Emphasis: Special attention is given to features that enhance your well-being, such as tracking your heart rate or setting up Fall Detection. You'll learn how to use these tools effectively, gaining confidence and peace of mind.

4. Breaking Down Complexity: This guide translates technical jargon into plain language, ensuring that the instructions are easy to understand and implement.

By the end of this guide, you'll have the knowledge and skills to use your Apple Watch Series 10 to its fullest potential. Whether it's staying active, monitoring your health, or keeping in touch with loved ones, this smartwatch is a tool that can truly enrich your life.

Chapter 1
Getting Started

Unboxing and Setting Up Your Apple Watch

The first step to enjoying your Apple Watch Series 10 is unboxing and setting it up. Apple has designed the unboxing experience to be straightforward and user-friendly, ensuring you can get started with minimal hassle.

When you open the box, you'll find your Apple Watch neatly arranged alongside the charging cable, power adapter (if included), and an extra watch band piece for size adjustment. Before proceeding, make sure you have your iPhone close by, as it will be essential for setting up the watch.

Start by carefully removing the protective plastic covering your Apple Watch. Once the watch is free, locate the side button and press it to power on the device. You'll see the Apple logo appear on the screen, signaling that the watch is ready to be paired.

Your Apple Watch will guide you through the initial setup process. Select your preferred language and region when prompted. If you have trouble reading the text, don't worry—accessibility features like Zoom or VoiceOver can be enabled later to enhance readability.

During setup, you'll need your iPhone. Ensure your iPhone is updated to the latest version of iOS to avoid compatibility issues. Place the watch close to your iPhone to begin the pairing process. The watch will display a unique pattern on the screen that you can scan with your iPhone's camera to establish the connection.

Pairing Your Apple Watch with Your iPhone

Pairing your Apple Watch with your iPhone is an essential step that allows you to unlock the full potential of your smartwatch. This process is quick and intuitive, designed to get you up and running in no time.

1. Automatic Pairing: When you power on your Apple Watch for the first time, a prompt will appear on your iPhone asking if you'd like to pair the watch. Tap *Continue*, and a pairing animation will appear on the Apple Watch screen. Hold your iPhone's camera over this animation until the watch is detected.

2. Manual Pairing: If the automatic prompt doesn't appear, open the Watch app on your iPhone. Tap Start Pairing, then follow the instructions to manually pair your device.

3. Sign In with Apple ID: Once paired, you'll need to sign in with your Apple ID. This step ensures your Apple Watch syncs seamlessly with your iPhone, allowing you to access features like iCloud backups, notifications, and more.

4. Choose Settings: The setup process will guide you through configuring settings such as location services, Siri, and Apple Pay. For seniors, it's a good idea to enable Fall Detection and set up Emergency SOS during this stage.

5. Syncing Apps and Data: Your Apple Watch will sync with your iPhone to download apps and settings. This may take a few minutes, depending on the amount of data being transferred. Keep the watch and iPhone close together during this process.

Once pairing is complete, your Apple Watch will display the home screen, indicating it's ready to use. Explore the basic features like notifications, messages, and activity tracking to familiarize yourself with the device.

Adjusting the Watch Band

Properly adjusting the watch band is crucial for comfort and accuracy. A well-fitted band ensures the sensors on the back of the watch maintain contact with your wrist, providing accurate health and activity data.

1. Selecting the Right Band Size

Apple includes two band sizes in the box—small/medium and medium/large—to accommodate different wrist sizes. Choose the size that feels most comfortable and secure. If you're unsure, try both sizes to see which fits better.

2. Attaching the Band

To attach the band, turn the watch over to access the release buttons on the back. Press and hold the button while sliding the band into the slot until it clicks into place. Repeat this process for the other side. Ensure both sides are securely attached before wearing the watch.

3. Adjusting the Fit

Once the band is attached, put the watch on your wrist. Slide the buckle or clasp to tighten the band until it fits snugly but comfortably. The watch should stay in place without feeling too tight. A proper fit is important for accurate heart rate monitoring and other health features.

4. Switching Bands

One of the perks of the Apple Watch Series 10 is the ability to switch bands to match your style or activity. To change the band, press the release buttons on the back of the watch and slide the band out. Replace it with a new band by sliding it into the slots until it clicks.

5. Caring for Your Band

To keep your watch band in good condition, clean it regularly. Use a damp cloth to wipe away dirt or sweat, especially if you wear the watch during workouts. Avoid using harsh chemicals or abrasive materials, as they can damage the band.

Unboxing, setting up, and adjusting your Apple Watch Series 10 are the first steps in unlocking its potential. By carefully following these instructions, you'll be ready to explore the watch's features and enjoy its benefits. With proper pairing and a well-fitted band, your Apple Watch becomes a comfortable, reliable tool that seamlessly integrates into your daily life. Whether you're tracking your health, staying connected, or simply telling the time, the Apple Watch Series 10 is designed to enrich your experience every step of the way.

Chapter 2
Understanding the Basics

Overview of the Apple Watch Buttons and Touchscreen

The Apple Watch Series 10 features a simple, user-friendly design that relies on a combination of buttons and a highly responsive touchscreen. Understanding these components is key to navigating your watch effortlessly.

The primary physical buttons on the Apple Watch are the Digital Crown and the Side Button:

- Digital Crown: Located on the right side of the watch (for most users), the Digital Crown is a versatile control tool. It allows you to scroll through menus, zoom in and out of apps, and even press it to return to the home screen or access Siri.

- Side Button: Just below the Digital Crown, the side button performs several important functions. Press it once to open the Dock, double-press to access Apple Pay, and hold it to use Emergency SOS or power off the watch.

The Touchscreen adds another layer of control. The Apple Watch screen is sensitive to both touch and gestures:

- Tap to select items, open apps, or confirm actions.

- Swipe left or right to switch between watch faces or other screens.

- Swipe up from the bottom to access the Control Center, where you can toggle settings like Wi-Fi, Do Not Disturb, or Airplane Mode.

- Swipe down from the top to see your notifications.

The combination of buttons and touchscreen gestures makes it easy to perform a wide range of tasks, whether you're checking notifications, adjusting settings, or navigating apps.

Navigating the Watch Face

The watch face is your Apple Watch's home screen, serving as the central hub where you can check the time, see widgets, and access shortcuts.

Switching Watch Faces:

To personalize your experience, you can choose from a variety of watch faces, each offering unique designs and complications (small widgets that display useful information).

- Press and hold the current watch face until it shrinks slightly, revealing the watch face gallery.

- Swipe left or right to browse available options.

- Tap Customize to adjust colors, styles, and complications for the selected face.

Using Complications:

Complications provide quick access to information or apps right from the watch face. For instance, you might see weather updates, your activity rings, or shortcuts to frequently used apps. You can customize these complications during the watch face setup process to suit your preferences.

Interacting with the Watch Face:

- Tap on complications to open the corresponding app.
- Swipe left or right to switch between your saved watch faces.
- Tapping the center of the watch face often provides more detailed information, depending on the design.

By tailoring the watch face to your needs, you can make your Apple Watch an efficient and personalized tool for daily use.

Understanding the Digital Crown and Side Button

The Digital Crown and Side Button are central to controlling the Apple Watch. Their intuitive design ensures you can navigate the device effortlessly.

Digital Crown:

The Digital Crown is more than just a button; it's a multifunctional control tool.

- Scrolling and Zooming: Rotate the crown to scroll through lists, adjust the zoom level in apps like Maps, or check activity details.

- Accessing the Home Screen: Press the crown once to return to the home screen.

- Opening Siri: Press and hold the Digital Crown to summon Siri for voice commands, like setting reminders or checking the weather.

The Digital Crown is designed to make navigation smooth, reducing the need to swipe excessively on the touchscreen.

Side Button:

The Side Button adds utility with its variety of functions:

- Dock Access: Press the side button once to open the Dock, which shows recently used or favorite apps. You can customize the Dock in the Watch app on your iPhone.

- Apple Pay: Double-press the button to open Apple Pay, allowing you to make quick, secure payments.

- Emergency SOS: Press and hold the button to activate Emergency SOS, which can call for help or alert your emergency contacts.

- Power Off: Hold the side button until the power-off slider appears, allowing you to turn off the watch or access medical ID information.

The Digital Crown and Side Button work together seamlessly, enabling a smooth and intuitive experience for navigating and controlling your Apple Watch. With a little practice, these tools will become second nature, making it easy to use your watch confidently and effectively.

Understanding the basic controls of the Apple Watch Series 10 is crucial for making the most of your device. The intuitive design of the buttons, coupled with the touchscreen's versatility, ensures seniors can navigate the watch with ease. Whether you're scrolling through apps, switching watch faces, or accessing emergency features, these controls are designed to be both functional and user-friendly. Take your time exploring the functions, and soon, you'll feel completely comfortable using your Apple Watch in daily life.

Chapter 3
Personalizing Your Apple Watch

The Apple Watch Series 10 is more than a tool—it's a reflection of your style and preferences. Personalizing your watch enhances both its functionality and your comfort with using it daily. This section will guide you through changing watch faces, managing complications, and adjusting display settings to make the Apple Watch uniquely yours.

Changing the Watch Face

The watch face is the first thing you see when you glance at your Apple Watch. With countless designs available, you can choose one that suits your mood, activity, or aesthetic.

How to Change the Watch Face:

- From the Watch Itself: Press and hold the current watch face until it shrinks slightly and a gallery of available faces appears. Swipe left or right to browse, and tap on a watch face to select it.

- Using the Watch App on Your iPhone: Open the Watch app, navigate to the Face Gallery tab, and browse an extensive collection of faces. Select one and customize it before syncing it to your Apple Watch.

Customization Options:

Most watch faces allow you to change colors, styles, and details like the type of clock hands or background imagery. Tap Customize on your watch to access these options. Use the Digital Crown to scroll through settings and tap to select your preferences.

Regularly changing your watch face keeps your experience fresh and allows you to adapt to different needs, such as a fitness-focused face during workouts or a minimalist design for casual settings.

Adding and Managing Complications

Complications are small widgets that appear on your watch face, providing quick access to information or apps. These might include weather updates, calendar events, or your activity progress. Customizing complications helps you access the information you use most frequently with ease.

How to Add Complications:

- On the Watch: When customizing a watch face, tap the area where a complication can be placed. A list of available complications will appear—select the one you want.

- On Your iPhone: Open the Watch app, select a watch face under My Faces, and scroll down to edit its complications.

Managing Complications:

- Rearrange or remove complications to focus on what's most important to you.
- Many third-party apps offer complications, which you can enable through the *Watch* app on your iPhone.

Adding the right complications to your watch face makes it a powerful tool for staying organized and informed.

Adjusting Display Brightness and Text Size

The Apple Watch Series 10 is designed to be highly accessible, allowing you to adjust display settings for optimal readability and comfort.

Adjusting Brightness:

1. Open the Settings app on your Apple Watch.

2. Tap Display & Brightness.

3. Use the sliders to increase or decrease the screen brightness.

A brighter screen is ideal for outdoor use, while dimming it can save battery life and reduce eye strain in low-light settings.

Changing Text Size:

1. Go to Settings on your watch and select Display & Brightness.

2. Tap Text Size and adjust it using the slider.

3. For more customization, enable Bold Text to make words stand out.

You can also adjust text size and bold settings through the Watch app on your iPhone. These settings are particularly helpful for seniors or anyone who prefers larger, easier-to-read text.

Using Zoom:

For those who need extra magnification, the Apple Watch includes a zoom feature:

- Open the Settings app, select Accessibility, and enable Zoom.
- Double-tap the screen with two fingers to activate the zoom, then drag to navigate the magnified area.

Personalizing your Apple Watch ensures it works the way you need it to while reflecting your personal style. Whether it's swapping watch faces to suit your day, setting up complications for quick access to vital information, or fine-tuning the display for easy readability, these adjustments make your watch more user-friendly and functional. Take the time to explore these settings and make the Apple Watch uniquely yours.

Chapter 4
Using Key Features

The Apple Watch Series 10 is packed with essential features that make communication, organization, and time management more efficient. Whether you're looking to stay connected with calls and messages, manage your schedule, or set reminders, your Apple Watch is an invaluable tool. This section will guide you through how to make the most of these key features.

Making and Receiving Calls

One of the most convenient features of the Apple Watch Series 10 is its ability to make and receive calls, directly from your wrist. Whether you're at home or on the go, your Apple Watch keeps you connected without needing to pull out your iPhone.

Making a Call:

- Using Siri: Activate Siri by saying "Hey Siri," followed by the name of the person you want to call. For example, "Hey Siri, call John Smith."

- Using the Phone App: Open the Phone app on your Apple Watch, then tap Contacts or Recent to find the person you want to call. Tap their name, and then tap the green call button to initiate the call.

Receiving a Call:

When you receive a call, your Apple Watch will display the caller's name or number on the screen. To answer, tap the green button, or raise your wrist if you have wrist detection enabled. To end the call, press the red hang-up button on the screen.

You can also adjust settings to switch between using the watch speaker or connected Bluetooth headphones for better sound quality during a call.

Sending and Reading Messages

The Apple Watch makes it easy to send and receive messages, even without needing to look at your phone. Whether through text, iMessage, or notifications, you can stay in touch with loved ones, friends, or coworkers with just a tap on your wrist.

Reading Messages:

Notification View: When you receive a new message, your Apple Watch will alert you with a vibration or sound. Swipe down on the watch face to view your notifications.

- Message App: Open the Messages app on your Apple Watch to see your full conversation threads. Tap a message to open it and scroll through the entire conversation.

Sending Messages:

- Using Siri: Activate Siri and say "Send a message to [contact name]," followed by the message you want to send.

- Dictation: Tap on the message field and speak your message. The watch will transcribe it into text.

- Pre-set Responses: You can also use quick reply options. If you don't want to dictate a response, choose from pre-set quick replies such as "OK," "On my way," or "See you soon."

The Apple Watch makes it simple to stay in touch, no matter where you are or how busy your day is.

Setting Alarms and Timers

With the Apple Watch Series 10, managing your time is effortless. Alarms and timers help keep you on track throughout the day, whether for waking up in the morning, cooking dinner, or tracking a specific task.

Setting an Alarm:

1. Open the Alarms app on your watch.

2. Tap Add Alarm and scroll to set the time.

3. Tap Set to confirm the alarm time.

You can set multiple alarms for different tasks, and you can turn them on and off from the Alarms app. The Apple Watch will notify you with vibration or sound when the alarm goes off.

Setting a Timer:

1. Open the Timer app on your Apple Watch.

2. Tap on the timer dial to set the duration of the timer.

3. Tap Start to begin the countdown.

You can start a new timer while another one is running, making it easy to manage multiple tasks at once.

Both alarms and timers on the Apple Watch are useful tools for managing your time and daily routine, especially when multitasking or staying on top of time-sensitive activities.

Using the Calendar

Your Apple Watch can act as your personal assistant, helping you stay organized and on top of your schedule. The Calendar app syncs with your iPhone's calendar, allowing you to view and manage your events right from your wrist.

Viewing Calendar Events:

1. Open the Calendar app on your Apple Watch.

2. You can scroll through daily, weekly, or monthly views to see upcoming events. Tap on a specific event to get more details, including the time, location, and any notes associated with the event.

Adding New Events:

While you can't create a new event directly on the Apple Watch, you can use Siri to add events to your calendar. Just say, "Hey Siri, add a meeting at 2 p.m. tomorrow," and Siri will confirm the event for you.

You can also receive notifications for events that are coming up, and your watch will remind you of upcoming appointments, meetings, and tasks.

The Apple Watch Series 10 offers a wealth of features that help you manage calls, messages, time, and appointments. By taking advantage of its communication tools like calling and messaging, time-management features like alarms and timers, and calendar integration, you can stay connected and organized with ease. These key features work seamlessly together, enhancing your productivity and keeping you on track throughout the day.

Chapter 5
Health and Fitness Features

The Apple Watch Series 10 is not just a tool for communication; it is a powerful companion for your health and fitness journey. Packed with innovative features to help you track your activity, monitor your heart rate, set fitness goals, and improve sleep patterns, it's designed to keep you healthy, motivated, and in control. Let's dive into these essential health and fitness features.

Tracking Your Steps and Activity Rings

The Apple Watch Series 10 features the Activity app, which helps you monitor your daily physical activity and encourages a more active lifestyle. One of the main components of this app is the Activity Rings, a visual representation of your daily activity.

Step Tracking:

Your Apple Watch tracks every step you take, from walking around your home to walking outside. The watch uses its built-in accelerometer to measure the number of steps, and it gives you a simple count that you can view at any time. It also syncs with the *Health* app on your iPhone for more detailed tracking over time.

Activity Rings:

The Activity Rings give you a clear view of your activity progress for the day. There are three rings:

- Move: Measures how many calories you burn through physical activity. The goal is usually set to 300 calories per day, but it can be adjusted based on your activity level.

- Exercise: Tracks how many minutes you've been active during the day. The goal is typically 30 minutes of moderate exercise.

- Stand: Tracks how often you stand and move for at least one minute each hour, with a goal of standing for 12 hours during the day.

Completing these rings is an excellent way to stay motivated. Your Apple Watch will send reminders if you haven't moved enough or if you're close to achieving your goals.

Using the Heart Rate Monitor

The Apple Watch Series 10 includes an advanced heart rate monitor, which measures your heart rate throughout the day. This feature can be useful for monitoring your health, especially if you're tracking your fitness or need to keep an eye on your cardiovascular health.

How It Works:

The watch uses photoplethysmography (PPG) technology, which uses light to detect blood flow under your skin. It takes measurements multiple times per minute, so you can monitor your heart rate in real time.

Checking Your Heart Rate:

To check your heart rate, simply open the Heart Rate app on your watch. It will display your current heart rate, and if you are engaged in exercise, it will also show your heart rate zone, helping you determine if you're in a fat-burning, aerobic, or maximum-effort zone.

Notifications for Abnormal Heart Rate:

The Apple Watch will send you notifications if it detects an unusually high or low heart rate that could be a sign of a potential health concern. This can be especially helpful for seniors or those with specific heart conditions.

Setting Fitness Goals

Setting fitness goals is a great way to stay motivated, and the Apple Watch Series 10 makes it easy to create and track your goals in the Activity and Fitness apps.

Setting Activity Goals:

You can customize your goals for the three Activity Rings based on your personal fitness level. To set your Move, Exercise, and Stand goals:

1. Open the Activity app on your watch.

2. Scroll down and tap Change Goals.

3. Adjust the numbers to your desired targets.

Your Apple Watch will then track your progress towards these goals every day, giving you motivation to move more and stay active.

Tracking Progress:

As you complete your goals, the Apple Watch gives you a daily summary of how you did. If you missed a goal, the watch will gently encourage you to do better the next day.

Sharing Fitness Goals:

For added motivation, you can share your fitness goals and progress with friends or family. You can invite others to be part of your *Activity Sharing* group, where you can compare your stats and encourage each other to stay active.

Monitoring Sleep Patterns

Good sleep is essential for overall health, and the Apple Watch Series 10 helps you monitor your sleep patterns to ensure you're getting the rest you need.

How It Works:

The Apple Watch tracks your sleep using a combination of sensors, including the accelerometer to detect movement and the heart rate monitor to monitor your breathing rate. It can tell when you fall asleep, when you wake up, and how many hours of deep, light, or REM sleep you get.

Setting a Sleep Schedule:

In the Health app on your iPhone, you can set a sleep schedule to help you get consistent rest. The Apple Watch will remind you when it's time to wind down and get ready for bed. It will also provide a summary of your sleep patterns the next morning, showing how well you slept.

Sleep Insights:

The watch will give you insights into your sleep quality, such as how much time you spent in each sleep stage (deep, light, REM), and provide suggestions for improving your sleep habits if needed. It's a great tool for seniors looking to improve sleep consistency and quality.

The Apple Watch Series 10 is a powerful tool for health and fitness tracking. With features like step tracking, activity rings, heart rate monitoring, personalized fitness goals, and sleep pattern analysis, it's designed to keep you on track with your wellness journey. By using these features, you can stay motivated, monitor your health, and make informed decisions about your fitness and overall well-being.

Chapter 6
Staying Safe with Apple Watch

The Apple Watch Series 10 offers a range of safety features designed to provide peace of mind, especially for seniors or those with health concerns. From detecting falls to providing emergency help, the Apple Watch can be a life-saving tool in critical situations. Let's explore how you can set up and use these safety features.

Setting Up Fall Detection

Fall detection is one of the most important safety features of the Apple Watch, especially for seniors or individuals at risk of falls. This feature uses the built-in accelerometer and gyroscope sensors to detect if you fall and automatically trigger an alert.

How Fall Detection Works:

When you fall, the Apple Watch senses the change in movement and orientation. If the watch detects a hard fall, it will automatically vibrate on your wrist and sound an alarm. After a fall is detected, you will have a few seconds to respond. If you are unresponsive, the watch will send an alert to your emergency contacts and share your location with them, ensuring they can assist you as soon as possible.

Setting Up Fall Detection:

To enable fall detection, follow these steps:

1. Open the Watch app on your iPhone.

2. Scroll down to Emergency SOS.

3. Turn on Fall Detection.

4. You can choose to turn on fall detection for all users or limit it to specific users (like those aged 65 and older, as fall risk is higher for seniors).

Fall detection can also be turned on directly from your Apple Watch by going to Settings > Emergency SOS and toggling Fall Detection on.

What Happens After a Fall:

If the watch detects a fall and you are unresponsive for a minute or more, the watch will automatically dial emergency services and share your location with them. It will also notify your emergency contacts. If you are able to respond, you can cancel the alert by tapping the I'm OK button.

Using Emergency SOS

The Emergency SOS feature on the Apple Watch Series 10 can be a lifeline in dangerous situations. This feature allows you to call emergency services with the press of a button, even if you cannot speak or access your phone.

How to Use Emergency SOS:

There are two ways to use Emergency SOS on your Apple Watch:

1. Press and Hold the Side Button:

Press and hold the side button (located just below the Digital Crown) for a few seconds. You will see the Emergency SOS slider appear on your watch screen. You can either drag the slider to call emergency services, or if you cannot swipe the slider, the watch will automatically call emergency services after a few seconds.

2. Automatic Calling:

If you press and hold the side button and do not release it, the watch will automatically dial emergency services after a countdown. You will hear a loud alert sound before the call is made. The Apple Watch will also notify your emergency contacts of your location and that you've called for help.

Sending Your Location:

When you use Emergency SOS, the Apple Watch will automatically send your current location to emergency services and your pre-set emergency contacts. This can be incredibly helpful in situations where you are unable to speak or provide your exact location.

Emergency Contacts:

You can set up emergency contacts in the health app on your iPhone. These contacts will be notified when you use the Emergency SOS feature. It's important to keep these contacts updated, especially if you have loved ones who need to be aware of your location in case of an emergency.

Health Sharing with Loved Ones

The Apple Watch Series 10 offers a feature called Health Sharing, which allows you to share your health data with trusted family members or caregivers. This feature is beneficial for seniors, as it lets loved ones keep track of your health metrics, such as activity levels, heart rate, and sleep patterns, even when they are not physically present.

Setting Up Health Sharing:

To set up Health Sharing, follow these steps:

1. Open the Health app on your iPhone.

2. Tap on your profile picture in the top right corner, then select Health Sharing.

3. Tap Share with Someone and select the person you want to share your data with from your contacts list.

4. Choose the health data you want to share, such as activity, heart rate, and sleep data.

5. Your family member or caregiver will receive an invitation to view your health data, and they can access it at any time.

Benefits of Health Sharing:

Health Sharing allows your loved ones to receive updates on your daily activity, heart rate, and other important metrics. This can be helpful for caregivers who are keeping an eye on your health or for family members who want to stay informed about your well-being. If something seems abnormal or if a health change occurs, they can offer help or encourage you to seek medical attention.

Privacy Considerations:

You control what information you share. The Apple Watch only shares data you've specifically chosen, and it uses encryption to protect your privacy. You can stop sharing data at any time, and you can choose to share only certain types of data, such as activity levels or heart rate, without sharing more sensitive information like medical conditions.

The Apple Watch Series 10 offers a comprehensive suite of safety features to ensure your well-being. With fall detection, Emergency SOS, and health sharing, the Apple Watch can provide life-saving assistance when needed and keep your loved ones informed about your health. By setting up and using these features, you can enhance your safety, improve peace of mind, and ensure that help is always just a button press away.

Chapter 7
Staying Connected with Apple Watch Series 10

The Apple Watch Series 10 is designed not just as a fitness and health device but as a powerful tool to keep you connected with the world around you. Whether it's staying in touch with family and friends, managing important notifications, or accessing useful apps, the Apple Watch ensures that you are always connected. Let's explore how to make the most of these connectivity features.

Using Wi-Fi and Cellular Connections

One of the standout features of the Apple Watch Series 10 is its ability to stay connected via both Wi-Fi and cellular connections. This allows you to use many of the watch's functions without needing to be near your iPhone.

Wi-Fi Connection:

When your Apple Watch is in range of a known Wi-Fi network (one that you have previously connected to with your iPhone), it will automatically connect to that network. This is particularly useful when you are away from your iPhone, such as when you leave it in another room or when you're out for a walk, but still want to receive notifications, send messages, or use certain apps.

Cellular Connection:

If you have an Apple Watch Series 10 with cellular capabilities, you can make calls, send messages, and access data even when your iPhone is not nearby. With cellular, you can stay connected wherever there is a mobile signal. This is perfect for individuals who enjoy going on walks or runs without carrying their iPhone, or for those who want the peace of mind that they can always be reached, no matter where they are.

To activate cellular, you need to set it up through the *Watch* app on your iPhone. Once set up, you can use cellular features, such as calling or texting, directly from your watch.

How to Set Up Cellular:

1. Open the Watch app on your iPhone.

2. Tap Cellular and follow the steps to activate cellular service with your carrier.

3. Once set up, ensure your Apple Watch has a strong cellular signal by checking the signal icon on the watch face.

Managing Notifications

The Apple Watch Series 10 makes it easy to manage your notifications so you can stay on top of important updates without feeling overwhelmed. Notifications alert you to messages, emails, calls, reminders, and more. With the Apple Watch, you can control exactly which notifications you receive and how they appear.

Customizing Notification Settings:

To manage notifications on your Apple Watch, you can adjust the settings in the *Watch* app on your iPhone. Here, you can choose which apps can send notifications to your Apple Watch. You can customize settings for emails, calendar alerts, social media updates, fitness reminders, and more.

How to Adjust Notification Settings:

1. Open the Watch app on your iPhone.

2. Tap on Notifications.

3. You will see a list of all the apps that can send notifications. You can choose to mirror your iPhone's notification settings or select custom settings for each app.

4. For each app, you can choose whether you want to receive notifications with sound, haptic feedback, or banners.

Managing Notifications on the Watch:

When a notification arrives on your Apple Watch, you can respond in several ways:

- Tap the notification to view it. Depending on the notification type, you might be able to reply to messages, dismiss reminders, or mark tasks as completed.

- Swipe down on the watch face to view recent notifications in the Notification Center.

- Clear notifications by swiping left on them and tapping Clear or Clear All.

The Apple Watch also allows you to enable Do Not Disturb mode, which silences all notifications and alerts. This is useful when you want some quiet time, such as during meetings, sleep, or while relaxing.

Accessing Apps from the App Store

The Apple Watch Series 10 supports a wide range of apps that can help you stay connected, be more productive, and enhance your daily life. You can access these apps from the App Store, which offers everything from fitness trackers to news readers, entertainment apps, and more.

Finding and Installing Apps:

You can browse the App Store for compatible Apple Watch apps either through the *Watch* app on your iPhone or directly from your Apple Watch. The *Watch* app on your iPhone provides a streamlined way to install and manage apps that are compatible with your watch.

To access the App Store directly on your Apple Watch:

1. Press the Digital Crown to go to the home screen.

2. Tap the App Store icon.

3. Browse or search for the apps you want to install.

4. Tap Get to download the app.

May apps that you use on your iPhone are also available for the Apple Watch, including apps for messaging, fitness tracking, music, weather, news, and more. You can also find new apps that are specifically designed for the watch's small screen and unique features.

Managing App Notifications and Settings:

After you install apps, you can choose to receive notifications for them and adjust settings within the Watch app on your iPhone. For example, you might want to receive alerts for your favorite news app, but not for every new game notification. Customizing these settings ensures that you only receive the most important updates, helping you stay connected without feeling overwhelmed.

The Apple Watch Series 10 provides multiple ways to stay connected, whether through Wi-Fi, cellular, managing notifications, or using the App Store. These features make it easier to stay in touch with friends and family, receive essential updates, and access the apps you rely on, all directly from your wrist. With these connectivity options, the Apple Watch enhances your ability to stay informed, entertained, and productive, while keeping you connected to the world at all times.

Chapter 8
Voice Assistance with Siri on Apple Watch Series 10

One of the most convenient features of the Apple Watch Series 10 is the built-in voice assistant, Siri. Siri allows you to use voice commands to perform a variety of tasks hands-free, making it easier to navigate your watch and complete everyday tasks. Whether you're sending a message, checking the weather, setting a timer, or asking for directions, Siri is your personal assistant right at your fingertips. Here's a guide on how to activate Siri, use common commands, and troubleshoot any issues you may encounter.

Activating Siri

Activating Siri on the Apple Watch Series 10 is simple, and you have several ways to do it, depending on your preference. Here's how to get Siri working for you:

1. Voice Activation (Hey Siri):

The easiest way to activate Siri is by using the voice activation feature. Simply raise your wrist and say, "Hey Siri." After a short pause, Siri will respond, ready to assist you with your request. Make sure that the Hey Siri feature is enabled in the Settings app on your watch. You can check this by:

1. Pressing the Digital Crown to go to the home screen.

2. Opening the Settings app.

3. Scrolling down and selecting Siri.

4. Ensuring that the Listen for "Hey Siri" option is turned on.

This hands-free method allows you to quickly access Siri without having to tap or press anything.

2. Manual Activation:

If you prefer to use a manual method to activate Siri, simply press and hold the Digital Crown until Siri appears on the screen. Once activated, you can speak your request, and Siri will process it. This method is useful if you're in a situation where saying "Hey Siri" might not be ideal, like in a noisy environment or when you need to conserve battery life.

Common Commands and How to Use Them

Once Siri is activated, you can use it to perform a wide variety of tasks on your Apple Watch. Here are some common commands and how to use them:

1. Sending Messages:

"Hey Siri, send a message to [Contact Name]."

Siri can send text messages or even iMessages for you. If you want to send a message to someone, simply provide their name, and Siri will ask for the content of your message. You can dictate your message, and Siri will transcribe it for you. If you're satisfied, you can confirm by saying, "Send."

2. Making Calls:

"Hey Siri, call [Contact Name]."

Need to make a phone call? Siri can place calls for you directly from your watch. Just provide the contact's name, and Siri will initiate the call. You can also ask Siri to "FaceTime [Contact Name]" if you prefer a video call.

3. Setting Alarms and Timers:

"Hey Siri, set an alarm for 7 AM."

"Hey Siri, set a timer for 10 minutes."

Siri can quickly set alarms and timers for various purposes, whether you need a wake-up call or a timer for cooking. Simply provide the time or duration, and Siri will confirm the action.

4. Checking the Weather:

"Hey Siri, what's the weather like today?"

Siri can quickly give you up-to-date weather information for your current location or any place you specify. You can ask for detailed information such as temperature, precipitation, wind speed, or the forecast for the upcoming days.

5. Checking Calendar Events:

"Hey Siri, what's on my calendar today?"

You can ask Siri to show your upcoming events, appointments, and reminders. You can also ask it to add new events to your calendar, such as: "Hey Siri, add a meeting to my calendar at 3 PM."

6. Controlling Music and Volume:

"Hey Siri, play some music."

"Hey Siri, increase the volume."

Siri allows you to control media playback and volume settings on your Apple Watch. You can ask Siri to play specific songs, albums, or playlists, or adjust the volume to your liking.

Troubleshooting Siri

While Siri is designed to work smoothly with the Apple Watch Series 10, there may be times when it doesn't respond as expected. Here are a few troubleshooting tips to help resolve common issues:

1. Check Your Internet Connection:

Siri relies on an internet connection to process commands. If Siri is not responding, make sure your Apple Watch is connected to Wi-Fi or has cellular service (if available). Without an internet connection, Siri may not be able to carry out commands like sending messages, checking the weather, or fetching real-time information.

2. Ensure Siri is Enabled:

If Siri is not responding to "Hey Siri" or the Digital Crown, make sure it is enabled in the settings. Go to the *Settings* app on your Apple Watch, tap Siri, and verify that both Listen for "Hey Siri" and Raise to Speak are turned on.

3. Check for Battery Saving Modes:

If your Apple Watch is in Low Power Mode, some features, including Siri, may not work as efficiently. Check your battery settings to ensure that Low Power Mode is not activated. You can disable it by going to *Settings* > *Battery* and turning off Low Power Mode.

4. Update Your Software:

Occasionally, software updates may address bugs that affect Siri's performance. Make sure your Apple Watch is running the latest watchOS version by going to Settings > General > Software Update.

5. Restart Your Apple Watch:

If Siri is still not working, try restarting your Apple Watch. To restart, press and hold the side button until the power off slider appears. Slide to power off, wait a few seconds, and then press and hold the side button again to turn your watch back on.

Siri on the Apple Watch Series 10 is a powerful tool that allows you to control many aspects of your watch hands-free. Whether you're sending messages, setting timers, or asking for weather updates, Siri can make everyday tasks much easier. By activating Siri, using common commands, and troubleshooting potential issues, you can enhance your Apple Watch experience and stay connected without needing to touch your watch.

Chapter 9

Customizing for Ease of Use on the Apple Watch Series 10

The Apple Watch Series 10 is designed with user-friendliness in mind, and it includes several features to help seniors and individuals with varying needs navigate their devices with ease. Customizing your watch for accessibility and simplifying notifications can greatly enhance the user experience, making it more convenient and intuitive. Below are some of the key customization options available to ensure that your Apple Watch is tailored to your personal needs.

Accessibility Features

The Apple Watch Series 10 comes with a wide range of accessibility features that allow you to tailor the device to your specific needs. Whether you have vision, hearing, or motor skill challenges, these features help ensure that you can use your watch comfortably and effectively. To access the accessibility options on your watch:

1. Open the Settings app.

2. Scroll down and select Accessibility.

Some of the key accessibility features on the Apple Watch include:

- VoiceOver: A screen reader that speaks the text on your screen aloud, making it easier for individuals with visual impairments to navigate.

- Zoom: A built-in magnifier that allows you to zoom in on specific areas of the display, helping individuals with low vision.

- Hearing Aids Compatibility: If you wear hearing aids, your Apple Watch can sync with them for a better listening experience.

- Sound and Haptic Feedback: You can adjust the haptic (vibration) feedback and sound alerts to suit your preferences, making it easier to receive notifications without visual cues.

Customizing these settings according to your personal preferences can enhance the experience and allow you to get the most out of your Apple Watch.

Enabling Zoom and VoiceOver

For individuals with visual impairments, the Apple Watch offers two essential accessibility features: Zoom and VoiceOver. Both can help make the watch interface more accessible and user-friendly.

Zoom

Zoom is a built-in magnification tool that allows you to zoom in on your watch display for better visibility. This feature is especially useful when you need to see small text or icons. To enable Zoom on your Apple Watch:

1. Go to Settings > Accessibility.

2. Select Zoom and toggle it on.

Once Zoom is enabled, you can double-tap with two fingers to zoom in on any part of the screen. To adjust the zoom level, double-tap and hold, then slide your fingers up or down to increase or decrease the zoom.

VoiceOver

VoiceOver is a powerful screen reader that provides spoken descriptions of what's on your watch's display. It's ideal for users who have difficulty seeing the screen. With VoiceOver activated, your Apple Watch will read aloud all on-screen text, icons, and even the names of apps. To turn on VoiceOver:

1. Open Settings > Accessibility.

2. Tap VoiceOver and toggle it on.

Once VoiceOver is enabled, you'll need to use a different gesture to navigate the screen. Instead of tapping or swiping normally, you'll need to tap the screen once to select an item, then double-tap to activate it. VoiceOver will announce each item as you move through the interface, helping you navigate with ease.

Simplifying Notifications

For seniors, keeping notifications manageable is crucial to avoid feeling overwhelmed. The Apple Watch allows you to control which notifications you receive and how they appear on your screen. You can simplify notifications to ensure that only the most important alerts are displayed, which can make the watch experience less stressful.

Managing Notifications

To manage your notifications on the Apple Watch, follow these steps:

1. Open the Settings app.

2. Scroll down and select Notifications.

3. You'll see a list of apps that send notifications to your watch. For each app, you can choose to allow or silence notifications, customize the alert style, or turn off notifications entirely.

To simplify notifications further:

- Set Do Not Disturb: You can enable Do Not Disturb mode to silence all notifications during specific times. This can be helpful if you prefer not to be interrupted or distracted.

1. Swipe up from the bottom of the watch face to open the Control Center.

2. Tap the moon icon to activate Do Not Disturb.

- Mirror iPhone Notifications: If you prefer to receive notifications from certain apps only on your iPhone, you can choose to mirror these notifications. This way, you won't receive duplicate alerts on both your iPhone and Apple Watch.

1. Open Settings > Notifications > Mirror iPhone Alerts From.

2. Toggle off the apps you don't want to mirror.

- Simplify App Alerts: For apps that you want to keep notifications from, you can adjust the notification style. Choose between Banners (which appear temporarily) or Alerts (which require action to dismiss). Banners may be less intrusive and easier to manage.

- Use Custom Vibration Patterns: If you prefer to receive a subtle notification, you can customize the vibration pattern for each type of notification, making it easier to differentiate between different types of alerts without needing to look at your watch. You can do this by going into Settings > Sounds & Haptics > Custom.

By simplifying your notifications, you'll reduce the number of on-screen distractions and focus only on what's important. This makes it easier to navigate your Apple Watch without feeling overwhelmed by too many notifications or alerts.

The Apple Watch Series 10 offers a variety of customizable accessibility options that can make it much easier for seniors to use the device. Enabling features like Zoom, VoiceOver, and adjusting notifications according to your needs ensures that your watch experience is as comfortable as possible. Whether you're enhancing the visibility of text, simplifying alerts, or managing the complexity of on-screen content, these accessibility features make the Apple Watch Series 10 a more accessible and user-friendly device for everyone.

Chapter 10
Maintaining Your Apple Watch Series 10

To ensure that your Apple Watch Series 10 remains in top condition and functions optimally, regular maintenance is key. This includes properly charging the device, cleaning it, and keeping the software up to date. By following these maintenance tips, you can extend the life of your Apple Watch and enjoy a better overall experience.

Charging and Battery Tips

The Apple Watch Series 10 comes with an efficient battery designed to last through daily use, but maintaining battery health is crucial for optimal performance over time. Here are some tips for charging and preserving the battery:

Charging Your Apple Watch

To charge your Apple Watch, use the magnetic charging cable that came with the device. Simply place the back of the watch onto the charger, ensuring the charging puck aligns with the magnetic connection. The watch will begin charging automatically, and the charging indicator will show on the screen.

- Charge Overnight: Many people find it convenient to charge their Apple Watch overnight, ensuring it's ready for the day ahead. However, be mindful not to leave it charging for excessive amounts of time after it's fully charged, as prolonged charging can gradually reduce battery life over many cycles.

- Avoid Charging in Extreme Temperatures: The Apple Watch's battery performs best in environments with temperatures between 32°F (0°C) and 95°F (35°C). Avoid charging it in areas that are too hot or too cold, as extreme temperatures can harm the battery.

Battery Tips to Extend Battery Life

- Enable Power Saving Mode: In low power situations, you can activate Power Reserve mode, which temporarily disables all non-essential features and displays only the time. To activate Power Reserve, press and hold the side button and swipe to activate the mode.

- Use Low Power Mode: For a more balanced approach to saving battery life, Low Power Mode reduces the device's background activities while keeping most essential features available. This is ideal for days when you need to conserve battery but still want the basic functionality of your watch.

- Disable Unnecessary Features: Turn off features such as "Hey Siri," background app refresh, and unnecessary notifications when not in use. These settings can consume power, so disabling them when they are not needed will help save battery life.

Cleaning and Caring for Your Watch

Regular cleaning and care will help your Apple Watch stay looking new and free from damage. The device is built to be durable, but gentle cleaning is recommended to maintain both the appearance and functionality of the watch.

Cleaning Your Apple Watch

To clean your Apple Watch, follow these steps:

1. Turn Off Your Watch: Before cleaning, power off your Apple Watch to avoid accidental inputs or damage.

2. Use a Soft Cloth: Use a microfiber cloth to wipe down the surface of the watch and band. Avoid using abrasive materials, as they can scratch the screen or body of the watch.

3. Clean the Display: If your Apple Watch screen has fingerprints or smudges, dampen the cloth slightly with water (never apply water directly to the device) and gently wipe the screen. Use a dry cloth to remove any excess moisture.

4. Clean the Band: Depending on the material of your watch band (silicone, leather, or metal), clean it accordingly:

- Silicone Bands: Use mild soap and water, or simply wipe with a damp cloth.

- Leather Bands: Clean leather bands with a dry cloth to avoid damaging the material. If necessary, use a leather cleaner.

- Metal Bands: Metal bands can be wiped down with a damp cloth, but avoid using any cleaning agents that could cause corrosion.

Caring for Your Apple Watch

- Avoid Exposing the Watch to Harsh Chemicals: Keep your Apple Watch away from harsh cleaning products, lotions, perfumes, and any substances that could cause discoloration or damage to the surface.

- Protect Against Scratches: While the Apple Watch Series 10 is durable, it can still be scratched. Consider using a screen protector or case if you want to add an extra layer of protection against scratches and dings.

- Water Resistance: The Apple Watch Series 10 is water-resistant (not waterproof), so you can wear it while swimming or during light rain. However, it's important to avoid submerging it in hot water or exposing it to other extreme conditions that could compromise its water resistance.

Updating watchOS

Regularly updating your Apple Watch to the latest version of watchOS ensures that you have access to new features, bug fixes, and security improvements. Here's how to update your Apple Watch:

Why Update Your Apple Watch?

Updates to watchOS often bring new features, improvements in battery performance, and bug fixes. Staying up to date ensures that your watch is operating smoothly, securely, and with all the latest functionalities.

How to Update watchOS

1. Ensure Compatibility: Before updating, make sure that your Apple Watch is compatible with the latest watchOS version.

2. Connect to Wi-Fi: Your Apple Watch needs to be connected to Wi-Fi to download the update.

3. Charge Your Watch: Make sure your Apple Watch is at least 50% charged or connected to the charger before starting the update.

4. Update via iPhone: The easiest way to update watchOS is through your iPhone:

- Open the Watch app on your iPhone.

- Go to General > Software Update.

- If an update is available, tap Download and Install.

5. Update Directly on Your Watch: If you prefer, you can update your Apple Watch directly:

- Open Settings on the watch.

- Tap General > Software Update.

- If an update is available, tap Download and Install.

During the update process, your Apple Watch will restart several times. Be patient and avoid interrupting the update.

Automatic Updates

You can enable automatic updates to ensure that your Apple Watch updates automatically when connected to Wi-Fi and charging. To turn on automatic updates:

- Open Settings on the watch.

- Go to General > Software Update.

- Enable Install Updates Automatically.

Proper maintenance of your Apple Watch Series 10 is essential to ensure it performs well over time. By following the charging and battery tips, cleaning your watch regularly, and keeping the software up to date, you'll extend the lifespan of the device and maintain its functionality. With a little care and attention, your Apple Watch will continue to be a reliable and valuable companion for years to come.

Chapter 11
Troubleshooting and Support

While the Apple Watch Series 10 is designed for ease of use and durability, there may be times when you encounter issues. This section will help you identify common problems, provide solutions, and explain how to reset your watch if necessary. Additionally, we'll cover how to reach Apple Support when you need expert assistance.

Common Issues and Solutions

Issue 1: Apple Watch Won't Turn On

- If your Apple Watch isn't turning on, here's what you can try:

- Charge Your Watch: Ensure that your Apple Watch is charged. Plug it into the charger and leave it for at least 30 minutes.

- Force Restart: Press and hold the side button and Digital Crown simultaneously for about 10 seconds, then release both buttons when you see the Apple logo. This can force a restart and resolve minor software glitches.

Issue 2: Apple Watch Not Pairing with iPhone

If your Apple Watch isn't pairing with your iPhone, try these steps:

- Check Bluetooth and Wi-Fi: Ensure Bluetooth and Wi-Fi are enabled on your iPhone.

- Restart Both Devices: Power off both your Apple Watch and iPhone, then power them back on.

- Reset the Watch: If pairing still fails, you may need to reset your Apple Watch (we'll cover this in the next section).

Issue 3: Apple Watch Battery Drains Quickly

A sudden drop in battery life can be caused by several factors:

- Check Background Apps: Close unused apps that may be running in the background.

- Turn Off Unnecessary Features: Disable features like "Hey Siri" or background refresh if they're not needed.

- -Low Power Mode: Enable Low Power Mode to conserve battery when necessary.

Issue 4: Apps Are Not Updating or Installing

If apps on your Apple Watch aren't updating, ensure the following:

- Check Wi-Fi Connection: Make sure your Apple Watch is connected to a stable Wi-Fi network.

- Free Up Space: If your watch's storage is full, delete some apps or media to create space.

- Reboot and Retry: Restart your Apple Watch and try updating the apps again.

Issue 5: Apple Watch Is Frozen or Unresponsive

If your Apple Watch screen freezes, try the following:

- Force Restart: Press and hold both the side button and Digital Crown until the Apple logo appear. This will force a restart and resolve most frozen screen issues.

Resetting Your Apple Watch

If you've tried the troubleshooting steps above and your Apple Watch is still having issues, you might need to reset it to its factory settings. This will erase all your data, so it's important to back up your watch before proceeding.

How to Reset Your Apple Watch

1. Backup Your Data: Ensure that your Apple Watch is backed up to your paired iPhone using the Watch app.

2. Unpair Your Apple Watch:

- Open the Watch app on your iPhone.

- Tap My Watch, then tap the i icon next to your watch's name.

- Tap Unpair Apple Watch. This will erase all data from the watch and return it to factory settings.

- During the unpairing process, your Apple Watch will automatically back up your latest data to iCloud or your iPhone.

3. Reset via the Watch: If you cannot unpair your Apple Watch via the app, you can reset the watch directly:

- Open Settings on your Apple Watch.

- Tap General, then scroll to the bottom and tap Reset.

- Tap Erase All Content and Settings.

- If prompted, enter your passcode and confirm the reset.

4. Set Up Your Watch Again: After resetting, your Apple Watch will restart as if it were brand new. Follow the setup instructions on the watch and the paired iPhone to configure it again.

- Important Note: A factory reset is a drastic step and should only be used if other troubleshooting steps haven't resolved your issues. Be sure you're ready to reconfigure your Apple Watch from scratch.

Getting Help from Apple Support

If the issue persists even after performing a reset or if you require expert assistance, Apple Support is available to help. Here are the ways to get in touch with them:

1. Apple Support Website

Visit the official Apple Support website (https://support.apple.com) for self-help resources, troubleshooting guides, and video tutorials. You can search for solutions to common issues or learn how to use advanced features of your Apple Watch.

2. Apple Support App

If you have an iPhone, download the Apple Support app from the App Store. The app provides easy access to troubleshooting steps, live chat, and appointment booking for repairs.

3. Chat with Apple Support

You can chat with an Apple Support representative directly on the website or via the Apple Support app. They can walk you through troubleshooting steps and help you resolve issues quickly.

4. AppleCare

If you have AppleCare+ or are considering purchasing AppleCare for extended warranty and support, you can contact AppleCare for priority assistance. AppleCare+ also provides coverage for accidental damage, which can save you money on repairs or replacements.

5. Genius Bar Appointment

If your Apple Watch needs in-person assistance, schedule a Genius Bar appointment at an Apple Store. The technicians there can help diagnose hardware issues, replace parts, or assist with repairs.

6. Phone Support

If you prefer speaking with someone over the phone, you can contact Apple Support by calling the toll-free number available in your region. Visit the Apple Support website for contact details specific to your location.

Troubleshooting your Apple Watch Series 10 can often resolve most issues with simple steps. Whether you're dealing with battery problems, unresponsive apps, or connectivity issues, these solutions will help you get back on track. In cases where the problem persists, resetting your watch or reaching out to Apple Support will provide the assistance needed to keep your Apple Watch in great working condition. With the right resources at hand, you'll be able to maintain your Apple Watch and continue enjoying its features with minimal interruption.

Tips and Tricks for Seniors

The Apple Watch Series 10 offers a wealth of features, and with a few helpful tips, seniors can make the most of these functionalities to enhance their experience. Whether it's optimizing battery life, using the watch as a remote, or discovering hidden features, this section will walk you through ways to get the most out of your Apple Watch.

Maximizing Battery Life

One of the key concerns for any wearable device, including the Apple Watch, is battery life. While the Apple Watch Series 10 offers an improved battery performance, there are still ways to optimize it to last even longer. Here are some tips to extend battery life:

1. Enable Low Power Mode:

If you're running low on battery, activating Low Power Mode can help extend usage. This feature reduces the number of background activities and dims the display. To enable Low Power Mode, open Settings, tap Battery, and toggle Low Power Mode on. You can also access it quickly by swiping up from the watch face and tapping the battery icon.

2. Reduce Display Brightness:

The Apple Watch display is bright and clear, but dimming it can save significant battery. To adjust the brightness, go to Settings, tap Display & Brightness, and move the slider to a lower setting.

3. Turn Off "Always On" Display:

The Apple Watch Series 10 includes an "Always On" display feature, meaning the watch face stays on even when you're not actively using it. Turning this feature off will help conserve battery. To disable it, go to Settings, tap Display & Brightness, and toggle off Always On.

4. Disable Unnecessary Notifications:

Constant notifications can drain your battery as the watch's display lights up each time you receive an alert. Go to *Settings* > *Notifications* and disable notifications for apps that you don't need alerts from.

5. Turn Off Background App Refresh:

Some apps refresh content in the background, which can be taxing on your battery. To disable this, go to Settings, tap General, then Background App Refresh, and select Off or Wi-Fi only.

Using the Watch as a Remote for Your iPhone

The Apple Watch Series 10 can double as a handy remote for your iPhone. Whether you're controlling music, taking photos, or finding your phone, the watch makes it easy to interact with your iPhone from a distance. Here are some ways to use your Apple Watch as a remote:

1. Control Music or Podcasts:

You can control your music, podcasts, or audiobooks directly from your Apple Watch. While playing media on your iPhone, open the *Now Playing* app on your watch. From here, you can pause, play, skip, adjust volume, and switch between tracks without needing to touch your phone.

2. Take Photos with the Camera Remote:

The Apple Watch can be used as a remote shutter for your iPhone's camera, making it perfect for group photos or selfies. Open the Camera app on your watch, which will display a live view of your iPhone's camera. Press the shutter button on your watch to take a photo.

3. Find Your iPhone:

If you've misplaced your iPhone, you can use the Apple Watch to help find it. Swipe up to open the Control Center and tap the Find iPhone button. Your iPhone will start ringing, helping you locate it, even if it's on silent mode.

Exploring Hidden Features

While the Apple Watch is packed with features, some of them are less well-known. These hidden gems can make a big difference in how you interact with the device, especially for seniors. Here are a few features you may not have discovered yet:

1. Walkie-Talkie Mode:

The Walkie-Talkie feature allows you to communicate with another Apple Watch user instantly, just like a two-way radio. To use it, open the Walkie-Talkie app, choose a contact, and tap their name to begin speaking. This is ideal for quick, hands-free communication with family or friends.

2. Siri Shortcuts:

Siri is great for hands-free assistance, but you can also create custom Siri commands to make daily tasks even easier. For example, you can create a shortcut to open your favorite apps or set a reminder by simply saying, "Hey Siri, remind me to take my medicine." To set up Siri Shortcuts, open the Shortcuts app on your iPhone and create commands that can be activated by Siri.

3. The "Taptic" Feedback for Alerts:

For seniors who might find visual alerts difficult to notice, Apple Watch offers haptic feedback. This means the watch will gently tap your wrist when notifications or alerts come in, allowing you to stay aware without looking at the screen. You can adjust the intensity of this feedback in Settings > Sounds & Haptics.

4. The Handwashing Timer:

A helpful and fun feature introduced in the watchOS 7 update is the handwashing timer. When you begin washing your hands, the watch automatically detects the motion and starts a 20-second timer, ensuring you wash thoroughly. You can turn this feature on in Settings > Handwashing.

5. Emergency Medical Information:

If you have medical conditions that should be accessible in an emergency, you can store emergency medical information directly on your Apple Watch. Go to Health on your iPhone, tap Medical ID, and add details like allergies, medical conditions, and emergency contacts. In the event of an emergency, first responders can access this information quickly by tapping your watch.

With these tips and tricks, seniors can maximize their Apple Watch Series 10 experience. Whether it's optimizing battery life, using the watch as a remote control, or discovering hidden features like Walkie-Talkie mode and handwashing reminders, the Apple Watch offers countless possibilities to enhance daily living. The key is to explore and tailor the watch to your specific needs, so you can enjoy all the benefits it has to offer.

Frequently Asked Questions (FAQs)

The Apple Watch Series 10 is a powerful and versatile device that offers a variety of features. Below are some common questions seniors may have about using the watch, along with answers to help make the experience smoother and more enjoyable.

1. How do I charge my Apple Watch Series 10?

Charging the Apple Watch Series 10 is simple and easy. The watch comes with a magnetic charging cable that attaches to the back of the watch. To charge it, simply connect the cable to a power adapter or a USB port on your computer, and attach the magnetic charger to the back of the watch. Ensure the charging contacts on the watch are aligned with the charger. You'll know the watch is charging when you see a green lightning bolt on the display.

For best results, charge your Apple Watch overnight, so it's ready to go the next day.

2. How do I adjust the font size on my Apple Watch?

Seniors may find it helpful to adjust the text size for better readability. To change the font size on your Apple Watch Series 10:

1. Open the Settings app on your watch.

2. Tap on Display & Brightness.

3. Select Text Size, then use the Digital Crown to adjust the size of the text.

This adjustment allows you to make the text easier to read based on your preference.

3. How do I activate Siri on my Apple Watch?

Siri is a helpful voice assistant that can be activated in several ways on your Apple Watch:

1. Say "Hey Siri": Simply speak the phrase "Hey Siri" near your watch, and Siri will activate.

2. Press and hold the Digital Crown: You can press and hold the Digital Crown (the round button on the side of the watch) to activate Siri if you prefer to manually trigger it.

Siri can help you send messages, make calls, set reminders, and much more, all without needing to touch the screen.

4. How do I set up Fall Detection?

Fall Detection is a valuable safety feature on the Apple Watch Series 10 that can detect if you've fallen and automatically alert emergency services. To set it up:

1. Open the Settings app on your Apple Watch.

2. Tap Emergency SOS.

3. Toggle on Fall Detection.

Once enabled, the watch will monitor your movements for signs of a fall. If the watch detects a fall and you don't respond within a certain time, it will automatically contact emergency services and send your location to them.

5. How do I pair my Apple Watch with my iPhone?

Pairing your Apple Watch Series 10 with your iPhone is a straightforward process:

1. Make sure your iPhone is running the latest version of iOS.

2. Power on your Apple Watch by pressing and holding the side button.

3. Hold your iPhone close to the watch, and the Apple Watch app should automatically open on your iPhone.

4. Tap Continue on your iPhone and follow the on-screen instructions to pair the devices.

Once paired, your iPhone and Apple Watch will sync, allowing you to receive notifications, calls, and messages on your wrist.

6. How can I track my heart rate using the Apple Watch?

The Apple Watch Series 10 features an advanced heart rate monitor that allows you to check your heart rate at any time:

1. Open the Heart Rate app on your Apple Watch.

2. Wait for the watch to detect your heart rate and display the results.

You can also check your heart rate through the Health app on your iPhone, where detailed heart rate data is stored. The watch continuously monitors your heart rate throughout the day and will alert you if it detects any unusual activity.

7. How do I change the watch face?

Changing the watch face is a fun way to personalize your Apple Watch. To change the watch face:

1. Press firmly on the current watch face to enter customization mode.

2. Swipe left or right to scroll through available watch faces.

3. Tap Customize to make adjustments, such as changing colors, complications, or other elements.

4. Once you're happy with the look, press the Digital Crown to set the new watch face.

You can also download additional watch faces from the App Store.

8. How do I update my Apple Watch to the latest watchOS version?

Keeping your Apple Watch updated ensures you have access to the latest features and improvements. To update your Apple Watch:

1. Ensure your Apple Watch is connected to its charger and has at least 50% battery life.

2. On your iPhone, open the Apple Watch app.

3. Tap General, then select Software Update.

4. If an update is available, tap Download and Install.

Make sure your iPhone is connected to Wi-Fi and your watch is in range to complete the update.

9. Can I use the Apple Watch without an iPhone?

While the Apple Watch Series 10 is designed to work in tandem with an iPhone, some features can be used without one. You can still track activity, monitor your heart rate, and use certain apps. If your Apple Watch has a cellular model, you can even make calls and send messages without needing your iPhone nearby, as long as you have an active cellular plan.

10. How do I reset my Apple Watch?

If you need to reset your Apple Watch, perhaps to fix an issue or before selling it, follow these steps:

1. Open the Settings app on your watch.

2. Tap General, then scroll down and tap Reset.

3. Select Erase All Content and Settings.

Be aware that this will erase all data from the watch, so make sure to back up any important information before proceeding.

The Apple Watch Series 10 is a user-friendly device with a variety of useful features. By following these answers to common questions, seniors can make the most of their Apple Watch, from basic setup to taking full advantage of health and safety features. If any additional questions arise, Apple Support is always available to assist with more advanced troubleshooting or guidance.

Conclusion and Final Tips

The Apple Watch Series 10 is an excellent tool for seniors, offering a blend of health and fitness tracking, connectivity, and safety features all in a sleek, easy-to-use device. By understanding the basics and utilizing the watch's key features, you can enhance your daily life, stay connected with loved ones, and even track your health and wellness with greater ease. The watch's intuitive interface, combined with customizable settings, ensures that it can be tailored to meet the specific needs of senior users.

In this guide, we've covered everything from setting up your watch to using advanced health monitoring tools like heart rate tracking, fall detection, and sleep analysis. We've also provided tips on personalizing your Apple Watch to ensure the text is legible, notifications are manageable, and settings are adjusted to your comfort level. Additionally, we've highlighted essential safety features, such as Emergency SOS and health sharing, which can provide peace of mind to both users and their families.

To make sure you're getting the most out of your Apple Watch Series 10, here are some final tips that can help improve your experience:

1. Stay Consistent with Charging

The Apple Watch's battery life can last up to 18 hours, but if you find yourself using the watch frequently, it's important to maintain a charging routine. It's a good idea to charge your watch overnight, so it's ready to go each day. If you're using more power-intensive features like GPS tracking or heart rate monitoring, you may need to charge it during the day as well. Consider setting up a designated charging station, such as by your bedside, to make it easier to remember.

2. Make Use of Health Features

The Apple Watch Series 10 offers a wide range of health features, including heart rate monitoring, fall detection, and sleep tracking. Take advantage of these to better understand your well-being. The watch can alert you to irregular heart rates, help you set fitness goals, and even monitor your sleep patterns to give you insights into your rest habits. Regularly check the *Health* app on your iPhone for detailed reports and progress.

3. Simplify Notifications

As a senior user, it's important to manage notifications so they don't become overwhelming. With Apple Watch, you can customize which notifications you want to receive. This can include everything from calendar reminders to text messages. By adjusting your notification settings, you can ensure that only the most important alerts come through, helping you stay focused without unnecessary distractions.

To manage notifications:

1. Open the Apple Watch app on your iPhone.

2. Tap Notifications and toggle the apps for which you'd like to receive alerts.

4. Take Advantage of Voice Assistance

Siri is one of the most powerful features of the Apple Watch Series 10, especially for seniors who may have difficulty navigating the touchscreen. With Siri, you can send messages, set reminders, make phone calls, or even get information just by asking. To activate Siri, simply say "Hey Siri" or press and hold the Digital Crown. This voice assistant can save time and effort, allowing you to manage tasks hands-free.

5. Keep Your Watch Clean and Maintained

To ensure your Apple Watch stays in good condition, clean it regularly. Use a soft, lint-free cloth to wipe down the watch face and the band. Avoid using harsh cleaning products or soaking the watch in water. When not in use, store your watch in a safe place, away from extreme heat or humidity.

6. Backup Your Data

In the event that you need to reset or replace your Apple Watch, it's important to back up your data. The watch syncs with your iPhone, so all of your health, fitness, and other data is stored in the *Health* app or iCloud. Make sure to periodically check that your data is being backed up automatically to avoid any loss of information.

7. Reach Out for Support When Needed

If you ever run into problems or need help with advanced features, don't hesitate to reach out to Apple Support. Whether it's through online resources, the Apple Support app, or over the phone, Apple provides excellent customer service and can walk you through troubleshooting steps. Additionally, the Apple Watch Series 10 has a helpful FAQ section and user guides on the Apple website to assist with any issues you may encounter.

In conclusion, the Apple Watch Series 10 is more than just a smartwatch—it's a powerful health, safety, and connectivity tool that can greatly benefit seniors. By following this guide and utilizing the tips provided, you can make the most of your Apple Watch, ensuring that it becomes an essential part of your daily life. With its intuitive design, customizable features, and helpful apps, the Apple Watch can help you stay connected, monitor your health, and navigate daily tasks with ease and confidence.